Family & Teen Cyber Safety Guide

Essential Tools and Tips to Protect Kids and Teens from Online Dangers and Digital Addictions

By Joe Correa

Published by Live Stronger Faster

This book is for educational and informational purposes only. The author and publisher are not engaged in rendering legal, financial, or other professional advice. Readers should consult a qualified professional before making any financial decisions.

First Edition

Table of Contents

Introduction

We are raising the first generation of children who have never known life without the internet. From the moment they can hold a tablet or smartphone, our kids are immersed in digital experiences that shape how they think, feel, interact, and learn. Social media, online gaming, streaming content, and digital school platforms are no longer optional — they're integral to the daily lives of children and teens worldwide. Yet, despite the convenience and opportunities these technologies provide, the internet has become a double-edged sword. With access comes exposure — to cyberbullying, inappropriate content, online predators, scams, misinformation, and the invisible trap of digital addiction.

As parents and caregivers, we often feel like we're racing to catch up. One moment we're learning how to turn off app notifications, and the next we're hearing about anonymous chat platforms, deepfake videos, or viral challenges that can lead to real-world harm. And with so many new platforms, features, and hidden dangers emerging daily, it's easy to feel overwhelmed and powerless. But here's the truth: you don't need to be a tech genius to protect your child online — you just need the right tools, mindset, and guidance. This audiobook is designed to give you that power back.

You are your child's first line of defense, and your influence is far more important than any app, firewall, or filter. That said, you need more than intuition. You need awareness of the risks that are often hidden in plain sight. You need strategies for setting boundaries that build trust instead of resentment. And you need practical solutions — from configuring parental controls to recognizing red flags — to help your child navigate a digital world filled with both wonder and warning signs. Think of this book not as a set of rigid rules, but as a flexible blueprint you can adapt to your child's age, personality, and unique digital life.

Our goal is to help you raise cyber-smart kids — not just kids who avoid bad content, but who understand how to evaluate information, protect their privacy, and recognize unhealthy patterns. Digital safety isn't just about avoiding threats. It's about building resilience, confidence, and healthy habits that will serve your child long after they leave the house. In the same way we teach kids to look both ways before crossing the street, we need to teach them to think before clicking, sharing, or trusting strangers online.

Throughout this audiobook, we'll break down the most common — and most dangerous — digital threats to families, including cyberbullying, sextortion, gaming scams, identity theft, and the darker corners of social media. But we'll also offer hope: real tools, real conversations, and real ways to empower your children to be safe, savvy digital citizens. We'll explore the latest parental control tools, but also how to talk to your child without creating fear or rebellion. We'll show you how to create healthy screen time habits, even if you've already fallen into a pattern of overuse or digital dependency. And most importantly, we'll help you model the kind of online behavior you want to see in your kids.

Digital parenting is not about constant surveillance — it's about active engagement. It's about creating a household culture where cybersecurity, digital respect, and open conversations are the norm. Whether your child is 6 or 16, it's never too early or too late to start. You can begin with small changes, build healthy boundaries, and create a tech-positive environment that supports learning, creativity, and connection — while still protecting against harm.

The online world can be dangerous, yes. But it can also be empowering, educational, and full of opportunities when used responsibly. Your kids deserve both access and protection. They deserve privacy and guidance. And they need you — now more than ever — to help them learn the digital life skills that schools often forget to teach. This audiobook will help you do just that, one chapter at a time. Let's begin.

Chapter 1: The Digital World Our Kids Inhabit

Today's children and teens are growing up in a reality where the internet isn't a tool — it's a world. Unlike previous generations who remember a time before smartphones, this generation has been immersed in digital environments since early childhood. From educational apps and YouTube Kids to online gaming and social media platforms, young people are living large portions of their lives online. And while many of these tools provide value, creativity, and connection, they also come with hidden psychological and safety risks that most parents aren't fully aware of.

Children as young as three are now regular users of tablets and smartphones. Many have YouTube channels, engage in gaming communities, and use voice search for schoolwork or entertainment. By the time they're pre-teens, they've likely been exposed to content — either intentionally or accidentally — that their parents would consider age-inappropriate. Whether it's through a TikTok "For You" feed or a friend's shared link, children are constantly encountering new media, and often, it's happening without adult supervision or context.

Social interaction has also shifted dramatically. Gone are the days when kids simply played outside after school. Today, friendships are built and maintained through gaming chats, Snapchat streaks, Instagram comments, and shared TikToks. Teens now communicate through disappearing messages, anonymous forums, and group chats where pressure to participate is high — even if the content is questionable. Many parents struggle to keep up with the lingo, trends, and apps their kids are using, creating a dangerous knowledge gap.

Understanding where kids spend their digital time is the first step in keeping them safe. Popular platforms among children and teens include YouTube, TikTok, Roblox, Discord, Snapchat, and Instagram. Each platform has its own culture, risks, and privacy settings — and not all are kid-friendly, despite appearances. For instance, Roblox might seem harmless, but its chat functions can expose young users to strangers. TikTok's algorithm can surface inappropriate or dangerous challenges. Discord, while useful for gaming communities, is often unmoderated and can expose teens to bullying, grooming, and adult content.

Another key concept to grasp is how tech is designed to be addictive. Many platforms are engineered to exploit dopamine cycles, triggering pleasure when a child receives a like, a comment, or wins a game. This can lead to compulsive behavior, anxiety when away from devices, and even withdrawal-like symptoms when screen time is limited. Social validation has moved online, and many kids measure their self-worth by their follower count or likes, often without realizing it.

Parents and caregivers must recognize that their child's digital life is real life. Dismissing it as "just screen time" or "just a phase" creates a communication gap. Instead, adults must engage with curiosity, not judgment. Ask questions. Sit beside them while they use apps. Watch the content they're viewing. Learn what the games are about. By participating in their digital world, you not only build trust but also gain visibility into potential risks.

The goal of this chapter is to shift your mindset: don't treat tech like a toy — treat it like a lifestyle. Just as you would teach your child to safely cross a street, you must teach them how to navigate apps, comments, messages, and media feeds. The earlier this education starts, the safer your child becomes. It's not about eliminating technology — it's about empowering children and teens to use it wisely, thoughtfully, and with guidance.

Ultimately, this chapter sets the foundation for everything else in this audiobook. Before we can protect, we must understand. And to understand, we must be willing to observe, listen, and learn from the very world our children are immersed in. The following chapters will guide you through practical tools and strategies, but it begins with one simple act: taking digital life seriously, just as our kids do.

Maria's story

Maria had always thought of herself as a pretty involved parent. She packed her kids' lunches, helped with homework, and even made a point to eat dinner together as a family most nights. But it wasn't until her 12-year-old son, Ryan, came home unusually quiet one afternoon that she realized something was wrong — and it had nothing to do with school.

After some coaxing and gentle prodding, Ryan finally admitted he'd been called names in a group chat on Discord during a gaming session. It wasn't just name-calling, either — it was targeted, hurtful, and it came from people he thought were his online friends. The worst part? Maria didn't even know he was using Discord. She thought his gaming was limited to playing Roblox and Minecraft. She had no idea about the private chats, voice messages, or the way kids could jump between groups without any adult oversight.

That night, Maria sat in bed scrolling through app store reviews and parental guides, feeling like a stranger in her own home. How had she missed this? When had digital life become so complex? As she explored more, she realized Ryan had accounts on TikTok and Instagram too. She'd heard the names before but never asked questions. She just assumed kids were being kids. She never imagined that behind those screens were entire ecosystems – places where reputation, social pressure, and danger existed in equal parts.

The more she learned, the more she realized how much she didn't know. TikTok wasn't just dance videos. There were viral trends, some encouraging risky behavior. There were filters that made kids question their appearance and anonymous comment sections that turned cruel in seconds. On YouTube, suggested videos could take a child from a harmless cartoon to an influencer promoting products or ideologies in just a few clicks. Even the games Ryan played had chat functions, friend requests from strangers, and in-app purchases disguised as "gifts."

But Maria didn't panic – she acted. She sat Ryan down and asked him to teach her about his digital world. At first, he was hesitant. But when she promised not to yell, judge, or take everything away, he opened up. They walked through each app together. They looked at privacy settings, blocked a few users, and set time limits. But more importantly, they started a new habit – talking about his online life just like they talked about school, friends, and feelings.

Over the next few weeks, Maria began to see digital parenting in a new light. It wasn't about control – it was about connection. She started sitting beside Ryan during his screen time. Sometimes they laughed at videos together. Sometimes they talked about things he'd seen that made him uncomfortable. It was eye-opening. She learned about slang, trends, and the emotional rollercoaster that came from being liked – or ignored – online. And Ryan? He began to feel safer, knowing his mom wasn't trying to spy on him, but support him.

Their relationship grew stronger, not because Maria banned everything, but because she finally understood the world he lived in. She saw it for what it was – a real place, filled with both magic and minefields. And she vowed to keep learning, listening, and leading, not from fear, but from love.

Chapter 2: Online Dangers for Kids and Teens

The internet is a powerful tool for education, entertainment, and connection, but it also hosts a darker side — one that parents can't afford to ignore. Children and teens are particularly vulnerable online because they are still developing critical thinking skills, emotional regulation, and judgment. Understanding the specific digital threats they face is essential for building effective safeguards and teaching smart decision-making.

One of the most common — and harmful — risks is **cyberbullying**. Unlike traditional bullying, which often ends when a child leaves school, cyberbullying follows them home. It can occur via text messages, group chats, social media comments, gaming platforms, or anonymous apps. What makes it even more damaging is its permanence and reach — hurtful posts or images can be shared instantly and remain accessible indefinitely. Children who experience cyberbullying may not always speak up, so parents must watch for behavioral changes such as sudden withdrawal, fear of going online, or anxiety around devices.

Online predators are another major concern. These individuals often pose as peers, slowly building trust before manipulating or exploiting a child. Grooming can happen in private messages on platforms like Instagram, Discord, Snapchat, or even Roblox. Predators may offer compliments, gifts in games, or shared interests to lower a child's guard. Over time, they may request photos, personal information, or even suggest meeting in real life. Teaching children about online stranger danger is just as important as teaching them not to talk to strangers in person.

Inappropriate content is also pervasive, and children don't need to search for it – algorithms may serve it automatically. Platforms like TikTok, YouTube, and Instagram often promote trending content, and some of it includes profanity, sexual themes, drug use, violence, or dangerous challenges. Even child-friendly apps can be gamed to display misleading or unsafe content through ads, clickbait, or loopholes in moderation.

Another hidden threat is **data privacy abuse**. Many free apps collect personal information such as location, device details, browsing behavior, and contacts. This data is often sold to third parties or used to build psychological profiles for ad targeting. Children unknowingly grant these permissions by tapping "Allow" without understanding the consequences. Parents must teach kids to read permission requests carefully and understand that "free" apps often come at the cost of privacy.

Scams and phishing attempts are increasingly targeting younger users, especially through gaming platforms and direct messages. Scammers might promise free game currency, exclusive items, or follower boosts in exchange for passwords or clicks. These schemes can lead to account theft, identity fraud, or device malware. Teens, eager for social validation or gaming rewards, may fall for these tricks unless they've been taught to recognize the warning signs.

Sextortion and inappropriate image sharing are some of the most serious risks, particularly among teenagers. Peer pressure, curiosity, or manipulation can lead to sharing private images, which can then be used for blackmail or spread without consent. In many cases, teens may feel ashamed or afraid to tell an adult. Creating an open environment where your child knows they can talk to you without immediate punishment is key to helping them recover if this ever happens.

Finally, **mental health impacts** are an under-discussed danger of online exposure. Constant comparison on social media can lead to anxiety, depression, body image issues, and low self-esteem. Teens may feel pressured to keep up appearances, post frequently, and gain likes or followers. This can create a false sense of worth and contribute to addictive behaviors or mood swings. As a parent, being aware of how digital content affects your child's self-perception is just as important as monitoring physical safety.

The purpose of this chapter is not to create fear — but awareness. Once you understand the potential threats, you're better equipped to teach your child how to recognize, avoid, and respond to them. Every danger discussed here can be mitigated with communication, boundaries, and ongoing involvement in your child's digital life. The internet is not going away. But with the right tools, your child can learn to use it wisely — and safely.

Now, lets talk about Tania and Emma

Tanya was thrilled when her daughter Emma turned thirteen and received her first smartphone. It was a big milestone, and Tanya felt confident she had prepared Emma well. They had talked about screen time, set some basic rules, and even installed a few parental control apps. Emma was responsible, smart, and kind — the kind of kid who seemed immune to online drama. But within a few months, Tanya began noticing subtle changes.

Emma, once bubbly and talkative, started spending long hours in her room with the door closed. Her laughter became rare. She seemed glued to her phone, often jumping to hide the screen when Tanya walked by. One night, Tanya heard muffled crying and gently knocked on Emma's door. After some hesitation, Emma opened up. She had been added to a group chat on a social media app where classmates shared cruel memes and messages about her appearance. It had been going on for weeks. She hadn't told anyone because she didn't want to make things worse — or lose her phone.

Tanya's heart broke. She realized that while she had covered the technical side of online safety, she hadn't prepared Emma emotionally for the darker parts of the internet. The next day, she sat down with Emma and listened. Really listened. Together, they reported the bullying, left the group chat, and blocked the offenders. But the damage to Emma's confidence had already taken root.

Later that week, Tanya checked Emma's other apps and discovered something even more unsettling. A stranger had been messaging Emma on Discord, pretending to be a 14-year-old boy who loved video games and animals — two of Emma's favorite things. The conversation had started innocently but had gradually shifted into questions about her personal life, her schedule, and even subtle suggestions about sending photos. Tanya intervened immediately, reporting the user and deleting the app. Emma was shaken — she had genuinely thought she was making a new friend.

That experience became a wake-up call. Tanya spent the next month learning everything she could about online dangers. She watched webinars, read parent guides, and joined a digital parenting group. She discovered the concept of grooming, sextortion, and how predators often use emojis and slang to avoid detection. She learned how some games had unmoderated chats and how apps could access Emma's location without her realizing it. She found out about scam messages disguised as giveaways and saw just how vulnerable even the smartest child could be.

Emma and Tanya began having weekly "digital talks" where they'd go through apps, review friend lists, and talk about what was trending online. Tanya stopped treating tech as a reward or punishment and started treating it like an ongoing learning experience. Emma, once hesitant, began to share openly again — sometimes even showing Tanya weird messages she received or TikToks that made her uncomfortable.

It took time, but trust was rebuilt. Tanya didn't shield Emma from the internet — she taught her how to spot its traps. They created a safe space where nothing was off-limits and no question was too embarrassing. Emma still used her phone daily, but now with a clearer understanding of what to avoid, who to trust, and when to ask for help.

And Tanya? She no longer saw herself as behind the curve. She had stepped up — not just as a mother, but as a guide through the tangled digital world her daughter was growing up in. Because in the end, it wasn't about restricting access. It was about building the confidence and awareness Emma needed to face that world — and thrive in it.

Chapter 3: Setting Boundaries Without Losing Trust

One of the greatest challenges parents face in the digital age is setting limits without creating rebellion. It's a delicate balance – you want to protect your child, but you also want to earn their trust. If the rules are too strict, they may sneak around them. If there are no rules, they may fall into risky patterns. The key is not just what boundaries you set, but how you set them. Creating a structure that feels fair, respectful, and collaborative is far more effective than rules imposed out of fear or control.

Begin by involving your child in the conversation. Instead of simply declaring new tech rules, ask questions that help you understand how they use their devices. "What apps do you use most?" "What do you like about them?" "Have you ever seen anything online that made you uncomfortable?" This opens the door to honest dialogue, rather than secrecy. When kids feel heard, they're more likely to cooperate with the limits you propose – and even suggest some themselves.

Boundaries should be age-appropriate, flexible, and focused on habits – not just time limits. While screen time caps (like 2 hours per day) can be helpful, it's even more important to define **when** and **how** screens are used. For example, no phones at the dinner table or after 9 PM, screens off during homework time, or only approved games during school nights. These guidelines teach structure and self-regulation while encouraging balance between digital and real life.

Another effective strategy is creating a **family tech agreement** — a written or verbal set of expectations that everyone in the home follows, including parents. This might include guidelines like:

- Devices are charged outside the bedroom at night.
- No secret accounts or anonymous apps.
- We talk openly about anything weird, scary, or inappropriate we encounter online.
- We treat others with kindness and report bullying or unsafe behavior.

This collaborative approach removes the sense of punishment and instead builds shared responsibility. Kids, especially teens, are more likely to respect rules they helped create.

Consequences for breaking boundaries should be clear and consistent but also restorative. Instead of just taking away a phone for a week, pair consequences with a conversation. "Why did you feel the need to hide that app?" or "What can we do differently next time so you feel safe talking to me first?" These moments are opportunities for teaching, not just punishing. If rules are enforced with understanding and fairness, trust grows stronger — even after a mistake.

It's also important to teach the **why** behind each boundary. Kids don't always grasp the real risks of unrestricted screen use, so explaining the reasons helps them buy in. For example:

- "We turn off devices at 9 PM because your brain needs time to wind down before bed."
- "We don't allow certain apps because they're not safe for your age group — they don't filter content or protect your privacy."
- "We limit time on social media because it can make people feel anxious or compare themselves unfairly."

Technology should not be treated as a reward for good behavior or a punishment for bad behavior. This creates unhealthy associations that can backfire. Instead, frame it as a tool — one that can be helpful, entertaining, or risky depending on how it's used. Teach kids to think critically about their own habits: "How do you feel after using this app for an hour?" "What do you wish you did instead?" "What helps you feel good online — and what doesn't?"

Above all, boundaries work best when there's **ongoing communication**. Set regular "tech check-ins" where you talk about what your child is doing online, how they're feeling, and what's changing in their digital world. Stay updated on new apps and trends, and be open to adjusting rules as your child grows. Boundaries are not static — they evolve with your child's maturity and your trust in their judgment.

Trust is earned both ways. When your child follows the boundaries you've agreed on, show appreciation and offer small freedoms as a sign of mutual respect. When they make mistakes, respond with patience, not panic. Your goal isn't control — it's to raise a child who can eventually set their own healthy boundaries, even when you're not there.

Jake's story on managing screen time

Jake was a typical 14-year-old — energetic, curious, and glued to his phone. His mom, Lauren, had tried setting screen time limits before, but it always ended in arguments. Jake insisted that his friends could stay up all night gaming or post on Instagram whenever they wanted. Lauren, worried about his grades slipping and mood swings getting worse, was ready to pull the plug completely. But something told her that taking the phone away wouldn't solve the deeper issue.

So instead of enforcing another strict rule, Lauren tried a new approach. She invited Jake to sit down at the kitchen table one evening, not for a lecture, but for a conversation. She asked him what apps he used the most and why. At first, he rolled his eyes, expecting to be scolded. But as she listened without judgment, he opened up. He told her how talking to friends on Discord helped him unwind, how funny TikToks made him feel connected, and how gaming gave him a break from stress.

Then, Lauren shared her side — not just as a parent, but as someone who cared about his mental health. She explained that she noticed he seemed tired, more irritable, and less interested in the things he used to enjoy. She didn't blame the phone — she just wanted to help him feel better. Together, they came up with a plan. No screens during dinner or in bed. Gaming was okay on weekends after homework was done. Social media time would be limited, and devices would be charged outside his room at night. It wasn't perfect, but it was a start.

They even created a tech agreement and pinned it to the fridge. Jake had input on every line. He suggested a once-a-week "no screen night" where they'd watch a movie or play board games together. Lauren agreed — and even promised to put away her own phone during those times. That night, something shifted between them. Jake didn't feel like he was being punished. He felt like he was part of the solution.

A few weeks later, Jake slipped up. He snuck his phone into bed and stayed up until 2 AM chatting in a group chat. When Lauren found out, she didn't yell. Instead, she asked, "What made you feel like you had to hide that?" Jake admitted he was afraid of missing out on a conversation his friends were having. Lauren nodded, then said, "That makes sense. But now you're exhausted — and I'm concerned. Let's talk about how we can do this differently."

They agreed he'd take a 2-day break from late-night group chats and find a different time to connect with his friends. He didn't like it, but he accepted it. The trust wasn't broken — it was tested and repaired. Lauren realized that the real win wasn't in controlling the tech — it was in keeping the lines of communication open.

Over time, Jake began managing his screen time more responsibly. He started noticing when certain apps made him feel anxious and began logging off voluntarily. He'd still slip occasionally — staying up too late or falling into a social media rabbit hole — but now he was more aware. And when he messed up, he knew he could talk to his mom about it, without fear of being shut down.

For Lauren, the victory was subtle but powerful. She hadn't just set boundaries. She'd built a bridge. A bridge made of trust, respect, and a shared goal: raising a teen who could handle the digital world with confidence, balance, and heart.

Chapter 4: Parental Controls & Monitoring Tools

In a world where children are more digitally connected than ever, parental controls and monitoring tools have become essential for helping families create safe online experiences. These tools are not about spying or removing freedom – they're about adding layers of protection, guidance, and visibility. When used correctly, they support the rules and values you've already put in place and give you peace of mind as your child navigates the vast digital world.

Let's begin with the basics: **what parental controls actually do**. At a minimum, these tools help you manage:

- Screen time limits
- App and game restrictions
- Web browsing filters
- In-app purchases and downloads
- Location tracking
- Social media activity
- Access to explicit or age-inappropriate content

Depending on the tool you choose, you can block specific websites, monitor keywords in messages, pause internet access at bedtime, receive alerts for risky behavior, and more. The right setup depends on your child's age, maturity, and risk exposure — and should always be paired with open communication.

Built-in parental controls are available on nearly all devices. For example:

- **iOS (iPhones and iPads):** Screen Time allows parents to set daily limits, restrict app access, and view usage reports.
- **Android (Google Family Link):** Offers screen time limits, app controls, approval settings for downloads, and GPS location sharing.
- **Windows and macOS:** Both offer parental settings to restrict downloads, web content, and screen time.

Many gaming consoles like Xbox, PlayStation, and Nintendo Switch also offer built-in controls to limit playtime, in-game chat, and spending.

For more advanced monitoring and filtering, **third-party apps** provide enhanced control. Popular options include:

- **Bark:** Monitors social media, messages, emails, and YouTube for signs of bullying, predators, or self-harm. Sends alerts, not full transcripts.
- **Qustodio:** Offers detailed usage reports, app blocking, screen time management, and location tracking.
- **Net Nanny:** Real-time content filtering, screen time schedules, and alerts for suspicious searches.
- **OurPact:** Great for managing screen time and scheduling device access.
- **Norton Family:** Includes robust web filtering and browsing history, ideal for school-age children.

Before installing anything, talk with your child. Explain that you're not trying to invade their privacy — you're protecting them from risks they may not yet fully understand. Make monitoring part of your **family tech agreement**, with clear boundaries and expectations. For example: "We use Bark to help catch things we might miss, but we trust you to come to us with anything confusing or upsetting."

Remember, monitoring is most effective when combined with **education and trust**. Tools can flag issues, but they can't replace your role as a parent. A well-informed child who understands how to use technology safely is still your best defense. Ask your child what features they think are fair or unfair. Adjust settings together. Review reports or alerts openly, using them as teachable moments instead of "gotcha" moments.

Also, keep in mind that **no tool is foolproof**. Kids often know how to work around filters or create secondary accounts. That's why **ongoing dialogue** is critical. Let your child know you're less concerned about mistakes and more concerned about helping them make safe choices.

Set a routine for **monthly reviews** of device usage, screen time patterns, and app activity. Make it a conversation, not a confrontation. Ask: "What app have you been using the most lately? Why do you like it? Are there parts of it that make you feel uncomfortable or pressured?" These check-ins reinforce your role as a guide, not a warden.

Finally, understand that your child will grow — and your tools should evolve. As they demonstrate responsibility, it's healthy to gradually loosen some restrictions and shift toward accountability rather than control. The goal isn't to monitor forever — it's to build digital responsibility so that your child eventually doesn't need constant supervision.

With the right combination of technology, conversation, and compassion, parental controls become what they were meant to be — tools of support, not surveillance.

Jayden's first iPhone story

When Melissa bought her son Jayden a new iPhone for his 11th birthday, she felt both proud and nervous. It was a rite of passage, one he had been begging for. She had done her research and enabled Apple's built-in parental controls — limited app downloads, blocked adult content, and set downtime hours. Still, a voice in her head kept whispering: "Is it enough?"

A few months later, that voice returned — louder this time. Jayden had started acting differently. He was more secretive, staying up late under the covers with his phone, always quick to change screens when someone walked into the room. Melissa, feeling unsure, decided to check the Screen Time settings. She was shocked to discover that he'd spent six hours on a messaging app she didn't even know he had downloaded — one that allowed anonymous chats.

It hit her like a wave. Jayden was smart, but he was also just a kid. He had figured out how to create a second Apple ID and bypass her restrictions. That night, Melissa sat on the edge of her bed, heart racing. She could yank the phone away. Ground him. Reset everything. But something told her that wouldn't fix the real issue.

The next morning, she sat down with Jayden and calmly asked him to walk her through what had happened. He confessed. A friend had shown him how to create a "backup" Apple ID to download games and apps without asking. He wasn't trying to hide anything — he just didn't want to be the only one in his group who didn't have access to "cool stuff." Melissa listened, breathed deeply, and then said, "Thank you for being honest. Let's figure this out together."

They decided to try a new system — one that gave Jayden some freedom but kept things transparent. Melissa installed **Bark**, explaining that it would notify her only if there were red flags, not every message. They reviewed the features together. Jayden even helped pick the settings he thought were fair. They turned off anonymous apps, enabled app approvals, and agreed to weekly check-ins — short chats where Jayden could share what he was doing online and ask questions about anything weird he came across.

At first, Jayden was skeptical. But over time, those check-ins became natural. He started telling Melissa about viral challenges at school and weird messages he got from strangers. When he stumbled on a YouTube video that made him uncomfortable, he came to her right away. Melissa realized that trust didn't come from watching every move — it came from **being involved without hovering**.

As Jayden matured, they revisited the settings. He asked to remove a few restrictions, and Melissa agreed — but only after they talked through the risks. One day, Jayden came home and said, "Some of my friends are using fake names online. That's not safe, right?" Melissa smiled. He was learning.

By the time Jayden turned 13, he wasn't just following the rules — he understood them. Melissa still used parental tools, but more as guardrails than barriers. And in the process, their relationship had grown stronger. She hadn't just raised a tech user — she was raising a digital leader.

Chapter 5: Safe Gaming and Social Media Habits

Online gaming and social media are two of the most popular digital activities among children and teens. They offer entertainment, connection, creativity, and even learning. But they also come with a range of risks – from cyberbullying to privacy violations, from addictive design to exposure to strangers and inappropriate content. Teaching kids how to use these platforms responsibly is critical for long-term digital well-being.

Let's start with **gaming**, which has evolved far beyond a solo experience. Most games today are networked, multiplayer, and come with built-in chat features. Games like Roblox, Fortnite, Minecraft, and Call of Duty allow players to interact in real time through voice, video, or text. While this fosters teamwork and community, it also opens doors to **toxic behavior**, **predatory contact**, and **unfiltered conversations**. Children may encounter inappropriate language, manipulation, bullying, or even grooming – all under the guise of friendly gameplay.

To keep gaming safe, parents should begin by researching any game their child wants to play. Look up the age rating, community reputation, and parental control options. Many games have built-in safety features that are often overlooked – including muting strangers, turning off chat, or disabling friend requests. Use these features to tailor the game environment to your child's age and emotional maturity.

Create a **gaming schedule** to encourage healthy time limits and balance with offline activities. Some families even use a "gaming license" model – a simple written agreement that outlines what's expected (e.g., being kind to others, asking permission before downloading new games, not chatting with strangers). Regularly review your child's gaming history and friend list. Ask them who they play with, what kinds of conversations happen, and whether they've seen anything that made them uncomfortable.

When it comes to **social media**, the stakes get even higher. Platforms like TikTok, Snapchat, Instagram, and YouTube are where kids build their digital identity. They share videos, post selfies, follow influencers, and interact with peers. But these platforms are also filled with **unrealistic beauty standards**, **viral challenges**, **explicit content**, and **cyberpressure** – the constant push to gain likes, comments, and validation from others.

Start by understanding the privacy settings of each platform. Sit down with your child and review their account together.

Make sure their profile is private, location sharing is turned off, and they're not accepting friend requests from strangers. Check if they're following or being followed by any suspicious or inappropriate accounts. Discuss the importance of not sharing personal information — like school names, phone numbers, or daily routines — in captions or messages.

Encourage your child to think before posting. A good rule is: "Would you be okay if this was shown to your teacher, coach, or future employer?" Remind them that the internet doesn't forget, even if something disappears in 24 hours. Apps like Snapchat and Instagram Stories can create a false sense of security — but screenshots and saved messages are always a risk.

One of the most overlooked areas is **mental health and screen comparison**. Talk to your child about how social media can distort reality. Everyone posts their best moments, not their bad days. Kids need help understanding that filters, follower counts, and curated content don't reflect real life. Encourage them to follow positive, uplifting creators instead of accounts that make them feel inadequate.

Gaming and social media shouldn't be viewed as "bad" — they should be approached like any other part of life: with intention and guidance. Ask questions like:

- "What do you enjoy most about this game/app?"
- "Have you ever felt uncomfortable while using it?"
- "Do you ever feel pressure to post or keep up with others?" These questions build digital awareness and open communication.

Most importantly, model healthy behavior yourself. If your child sees you scrolling endlessly, checking likes, or responding to every notification during dinner, they'll learn to do the same. Show them how you manage digital life with boundaries and self-respect. Technology isn't going away — but with the right habits, it can enhance, not harm, your child's development.

Now, lets go over Lena's story

Lena's son Mateo loved video games. From the moment he got home from school, he'd rush to his room, headset on, controller in hand, laughing and shouting as he played with his online friends. Lena didn't mind at first. It seemed like harmless fun — a way to unwind after class. But after a few months, she noticed changes. Mateo was staying up too late, snapping at his little sister, and getting frustrated whenever she asked him to take a break.

One night, after hearing him yell angrily through the walls, Lena peeked into his room. Mateo quickly pulled off his headset and tried to change the subject, but she caught a glimpse of the game's chat screen. It wasn't just friendly banter — it was filled with insults, threats, and pressure to keep playing. The next morning, she sat down with him over breakfast and gently asked, "What's been going on in your games lately?"

Mateo sighed. "It's just part of how people talk online. If you leave, they call you weak. If you don't respond, they kick you from the group." It hit Lena hard. She realized he wasn't just playing games — he was navigating an unfiltered social world, full of its own rules, hierarchies, and dangers.

That weekend, Lena took a deep dive into gaming safety. She learned how to adjust settings to block unknown players, mute toxic chats, and report harassment. But more importantly, she talked to Mateo about how the games made him feel. Together, they created a "gaming code" — rules about who he could play with, how late he could stay up, and what to do if someone crossed the line. Mateo, to her surprise, appreciated it. He'd been feeling stressed but didn't know how to ask for help without losing access to something he enjoyed.

Not long after, Mateo joined Instagram. Lena was hesitant. She'd heard stories about bullying, predators, and dangerous trends. But she didn't want to ban it outright — she wanted to learn. So she asked Mateo to show her the app. They sat side-by-side on the couch, scrolling through his feed. He showed her the accounts he followed, the videos he liked, and some of the messages he received. One comment from a stranger stood out — it seemed harmless but a little too personal. Lena pointed it out, and Mateo agreed to block the user.

They went over his privacy settings together. They turned off location tracking, made his profile private, and removed a few followers he didn't recognize. Lena reminded him not to post pictures with his school name, license plate, or house in the background. "Even small details," she said, "can tell someone too much."

Over time, Mateo began making smarter choices. He skipped certain online challenges that made him uncomfortable. He started following more positive creators — people who made him laugh or taught him something new. And every so often, he'd hand Lena his phone and ask, "Do you think this post is okay?" She never judged. She offered guidance.

Their bond deepened – not just because Lena had set rules, but because she stayed engaged. She didn't treat gaming or social media as problems to fix. She treated them as parts of Mateo's world – places he needed her help to explore safely. And Mateo? He didn't just become a better gamer or smarter poster. He became more aware, more confident, and more in control of his own digital choices.

Chapter 6: Teaching Critical Thinking & Digital Literacy

In a world flooded with information, teaching children and teens how to think critically online is not optional — it's essential. Digital literacy goes far beyond knowing how to use a device. It means being able to evaluate the credibility of information, identify manipulation, recognize scams, and make smart, safe choices in a complex and constantly changing online environment.

Many young people today can navigate an app with ease, but struggle to tell the difference between a sponsored post and a real recommendation, or between an opinion and a verified fact. Algorithms serve up a constant stream of curated content — much of it designed to grab attention, provoke emotion, or sell something. Without digital literacy, children are vulnerable to misinformation, online traps, and distorted worldviews.

Start with the basics: teach your child to **question what they see**. Ask them to think about who created a piece of content, why they created it, and what the goal is. Is the video trying to inform, persuade, entertain, or manipulate? Encourage questions like:

- "Who benefits from this post going viral?"
- "Is this a trusted source or just someone's opinion?"
- "Does this image look edited or out of context?"

When kids learn to ask these questions, they develop mental filters that help them separate real from fake — something even many adults struggle with.

Scams and **phishing attempts** are increasingly targeting younger users. These may come in the form of fake giveaways, suspicious links, "get-rich-quick" messages, or impersonators pretending to be friends. Teach your child that if something seems too good to be true, it probably is. Show them how to spot red flags like urgent language ("Act now!"), grammar mistakes, or requests for personal information. Practice role-playing scenarios so they know how to respond when approached by a stranger online.

Next, explain the concept of **digital permanence**. Help them understand that once something is posted, even if it's deleted, it can be saved, screenshot, or shared without their control. Teach them to think long-term: would they be okay with a post resurfacing in 10 years? Encourage them to avoid sharing sensitive photos, private information, or emotionally charged reactions that could later be used against them.

Passwords are another key part of digital literacy. Many kids reuse the same password across multiple platforms or use simple combinations that are easy to guess. Teach them how to create strong passwords and why they should never share them — not even with friends. Introduce them to password managers if age-appropriate, or encourage writing passwords down in a secure physical place.

Also, teach the **difference between private and public conversations**. Messaging apps, group chats, and forums may feel private, but many are not encrypted or secure. Kids should know that anything they type could be seen, recorded, or leaked. Help them understand that being anonymous online doesn't make them invisible — and it certainly doesn't make them invincible.

Another important aspect of digital literacy is **emotional regulation**. Many platforms are designed to provoke reactions — anger, jealousy, outrage — to keep users engaged. Teach kids to pause before replying, clicking, or sharing. If something makes them feel upset or confused, encourage them to talk it through with a trusted adult. Help them recognize how their mood can be influenced by online content — and when to log off to protect their mental space.

Incorporate digital literacy into everyday life. Watch videos together and discuss whether they seem credible. Show them how to fact-check using reliable sources. Look at influencer posts and talk about marketing tactics. When you make decisions based on online research — like reviews or news — explain your process. You're not just guiding their actions; you're modeling how to think.

Finally, reward curiosity. When your child brings you a strange post, a confusing message, or an unbelievable claim and asks, "Is this true?", celebrate that moment. That question is the beginning of critical thinking — and the most powerful defense your child will ever have in a digital world that isn't always what it seems.

The story of Ava and the $10,000 vieo

Twelve-year-old Ava was sitting on the couch, scrolling through TikTok, when she gasped. "Mom, look! This guy says you can make $10,000 in one day just by clicking a link and watching videos!" Her mom, Rachel, peeked over and raised an eyebrow. The video was flashy — lots of cash, big promises, and a fast-talking influencer claiming he had a secret method. Ava was intrigued. Rachel was concerned.

Instead of dismissing it immediately, Rachel sat beside her and said, "Let's look at it together." They rewatched the video, this time pausing every few seconds. "Did you notice how many times he said 'trust me'?" Rachel asked. "Or how he never actually explained how it works?" Ava nodded. "Yeah... and the comments are turned off."

That evening, Rachel showed Ava how to reverse-image search photos and look up user profiles. They found out the account had only been active for a week and had dozens of identical posts with different faces and names — a clear scam strategy. Ava was amazed. "I had no idea people faked stuff like this just for views," she said. "I thought TikTok had rules." Rachel replied, "It does, but not everything gets caught in time. That's why it's important to look carefully."

A few days later, Ava received a message on her gaming platform offering her free in-game currency in exchange for her login info. Remembering what she'd learned, she ignored the message and came straight to Rachel. Together, they reported the user and changed Ava's password just in case. Rachel used the moment to explain how scammers often pretend to be game developers or popular players to trick people.

Soon, Ava was spotting sketchy stuff on her own. When her friend Mia forwarded a "celebrity giveaway" post that promised a free iPhone, Ava replied, "It's fake — look at the spelling and the profile picture. That account has no blue checkmark." She started becoming the "digital detective" in her friend group — questioning trends, checking sources, and even teaching her classmates how to spot fake news.

One afternoon, Ava came home excited. "We talked about deepfakes in school today! But I already knew about them because of our talks." Rachel smiled. They had watched a video together weeks earlier that showed how realistic AI-generated faces could be. They had talked about how scary — and fascinating — it was that someone could appear to say something they never actually said. Now, Ava felt prepared, not paranoid.

Their conversations became routine. When Ava wanted to download a new app, they reviewed the permissions together. When a video upset her, they talked about why it triggered her and whether it was manipulative. Rachel never judged or overreacted — she helped Ava think it through. Over time, Ava's instincts sharpened. She started asking questions out loud before clicking anything: "What's the motive here? Who made this? Could this be fake?"

One evening, as Rachel scrolled through social media herself, she paused and showed Ava a headline: "Aliens confirmed by leaked NASA footage." Ava raised an eyebrow. "That font is classic clickbait. And the website name sounds like a joke." Rachel laughed. "You're rubbing off on me."

By guiding Ava through the digital jungle with curiosity and critical thinking, Rachel had done something more powerful than setting rules — she'd built a filter in her daughter's mind. A filter that questioned, analyzed, and understood. A filter that would protect Ava, long after the parental controls were gone. A filter no one could hack.

Chapter 7: Managing Screen Addiction and Digital Burnout

Screen addiction is a modern epidemic — and it's affecting children and teens more than any other age group. While devices are essential for school, communication, and entertainment, excessive use can lead to sleep disturbances, reduced academic performance, emotional dysregulation, and even physical health issues like poor posture and eye strain. But the deeper issue is often psychological: dependency on digital stimulation, social validation, and instant gratification.

Understanding the science behind screen addiction helps parents respond with empathy rather than frustration. Most apps and games are intentionally designed to be addictive. Features like endless scrolling, autoplay, push notifications, and reward loops trigger dopamine responses in the brain — the same chemical released during pleasurable activities like eating or winning. For developing brains, this feedback loop can be especially powerful, training kids to crave the next "hit" from a like, a message, or a win in a game.

The first step in managing screen addiction is recognizing the **warning signs**. These may include:

- Irritability or anxiety when separated from devices

- Loss of interest in offline activities
- Sneaking screen time or lying about usage
- Trouble sleeping or waking up tired despite long hours in bed
- Difficulty focusing or completing tasks without checking a device

Once you've identified potential overuse, resist the urge to blame or punish. Instead, open a conversation: "I've noticed you seem more tired lately – could it be related to how late you're on your phone?" or "You used to love playing outside after school – is there something about screens that's replacing that?"

Create a **tech balance plan** that supports moderation rather than forced deprivation. This includes:

- **Tech-free zones and times** (e.g., bedrooms, dinner table, family outings)
- **Scheduled screen time** for leisure use, separate from school-related use

- **Alternative activities** like board games, sports, creative hobbies, or social events that don't involve screens
- **Device curfews**, such as no screens an hour before bedtime

Be transparent about **why** limits are needed. For example:

- "Screens before bed interfere with your brain's ability to fall asleep."
- "Taking breaks from devices improves focus and energy."
- "Our minds need offline time to reset and process the day."

Modeling healthy digital behavior as a parent is one of the most effective strategies. Children watch how adults use technology. If they see you glued to your phone during dinner or reaching for it first thing in the morning, they will adopt similar habits. Demonstrate self-control by setting your own boundaries — such as putting your phone away during family time or using screen time trackers.

Consider **digital detox challenges** as a family. Try a "No-Screen Sunday" or a tech-free evening once a week. Turn it into a fun ritual: play a card game, go for a walk, bake together, or read aloud. When digital breaks are enjoyable and consistent, they help rewire the brain to find pleasure in real-world experiences again.

Technology isn't going away, and it shouldn't be feared. The goal is to **build digital resilience** – the ability to enjoy and benefit from tech without becoming dependent on it. For some children, you may also need to explore underlying causes. Is your child escaping boredom, stress, or loneliness through screens? If so, address the root issue with care and, if necessary, involve a counselor or mental health professional.

Lastly, track your progress without obsessing. Use screen time reports from your child's device to notice patterns and improvements. Celebrate small wins like "3 days without using devices before bed" or "replacing one hour of scrolling with drawing or reading." These shifts, over time, create lasting change.

Managing screen addiction is not about taking something away – it's about giving something back: rest, focus, connection, creativity, and peace of mind.

The story of Zoe's late night smartphone use

Every night, around 10 p.m., Lisa would walk past her daughter's room and see the glow of a screen through the cracked door. Twelve-year-old Zoe was supposed to be asleep by 9:30, but more often than not, she was buried in TikTok videos, laughing quietly, her eyes wide with stimulation. In the mornings, Zoe was groggy, irritable, and distracted. Homework went unfinished. Family meals were silent. Something had shifted.

Lisa knew Zoe loved her phone — it was her main connection to friends, school updates, and her favorite influencers. But what began as fun was starting to feel like a dependency. One night, after Zoe snapped at her for asking a simple question, Lisa decided to have a heart-to-heart.

Instead of scolding, she sat beside her daughter and said, "I've noticed you're not your usual self lately. Can we talk about how much you're using your phone at night?" Zoe didn't answer at first, but after a long pause, she whispered, "I can't sleep without it. It's like... my brain won't shut off." Lisa felt a wave of compassion. Her daughter wasn't misbehaving — she was overwhelmed.

The next day, they made a plan together. They created a small basket in the kitchen where all devices would go at 9 p.m. —

including Lisa's. "If we both do it, it'll be easier," she promised. They bought a fun alarm clock so Zoe wouldn't need her phone in bed, and they made a checklist of relaxing activities to do before sleep: stretch, journal, read, listen to calming music.

The first few nights were hard. Zoe kept reaching for her phantom phone. But by the end of the week, she admitted she felt better in the mornings. Her mood improved. She laughed more. She started doodling again — something she hadn't done in months.

They also implemented "Tech-Free Tuesdays." Every week, after dinner, the whole family would put away their devices for two hours. At first, it felt awkward — staring at each other without screens. But then they started playing card games, cooking new recipes, and telling stories. It became a favorite family ritual.

Lisa took it a step further and downloaded a screen time tracker on both their phones. They checked the numbers together on Sunday nights. "Wow, you were on YouTube for five hours on Friday?" Lisa would say with a smile, not judgment. Zoe would roll her eyes and laugh, "Okay, okay — I'll chill this week." They began to treat it like a game — a way to stay mindful, not a way to shame.

Zoe started setting her own boundaries. She removed a few apps she found too addictive. She muted notifications during school hours. She even convinced two of her friends to try "Phone-Free Fridays." The difference in her energy, focus, and creativity was undeniable.

One evening, Zoe sat on the porch with her sketchpad, drawing quietly. Lisa sat beside her, phone-free, just enjoying the breeze. Zoe turned and said, "It's weird. I used to think being offline would make me bored. But it actually feels kind of... peaceful."

Lisa smiled. "That's the magic of balance."

Chapter 8: Building a Long-Term Cyber Safety Culture at Home

Protecting children and teens online isn't about one-time settings or isolated conversations — it's about cultivating a long-term *cyber safety culture* at home. This means creating a household environment where cybersecurity, privacy, balance, and communication are ongoing values practiced by everyone — not just rules imposed on kids. When families treat digital awareness like they do brushing teeth or buckling a seatbelt, it becomes second nature.

The foundation of this culture is **consistent communication**. Cyber safety should be a regular topic, not something that only comes up when a problem arises. Schedule monthly or bi-weekly "digital check-ins" to review new apps, recent activity, changing interests, or updates to family tech rules. Ask open-ended questions:

- "What's your favorite app right now and why?"
- "Have you seen anything online that seemed strange or made you uncomfortable?"
- "Are there any new trends or slang words I should know about?"

The key is to stay curious, not critical. Your goal is to create an atmosphere where kids feel safe discussing their digital lives – including mistakes. Let them know that if they ever click something dangerous, receive a creepy message, or get caught in drama, they can come to you without fear of being punished or judged.

Next, update your **tech rules and boundaries as kids grow**. What's appropriate for a 9-year-old won't work for a 14-year-old. As they mature, involve them in setting their own limits. This teaches responsibility and helps them understand the reasoning behind safety measures. For example, you might allow a teen to use certain social media apps with monitored usage and regular reviews, while a younger child may only be allowed to use curated platforms with strict parental controls.

Make **cyber safety a shared value**, not just a parental rule. Let your kids see you using privacy tools like password managers, multi-factor authentication, and VPNs. Talk about how you handle spam emails, phishing attempts, and suspicious links. When your kids see that even adults have to stay vigilant, it normalizes the idea that digital safety is a lifelong habit.

One powerful strategy is to create a **"Family Digital Charter"** – a visible list of digital values and agreements posted in a common area. This can include items like:

- We talk openly about our online experiences.
- We take breaks from screens to enjoy time offline.
- We don't share private information without thinking.
- We ask before posting pictures of family members.
- We report anything unsafe or unkind we see online.

Reinforce these principles through **positive reinforcement**. Praise your child when they make smart choices, like ignoring a spam message or helping a friend with a privacy setting. Celebrate digital wins the same way you would academic or sports achievements.

Also, **stay informed**. Subscribe to newsletters from online safety organizations, attend school webinars, or follow digital parenting experts. Tech evolves fast – new apps, games, and scams pop up weekly. A family culture of safety means you keep learning and adapting together.

Include cyber safety in **life skills education**. Just as you teach kids about money, relationships, or cooking, make sure they understand data privacy, scam detection, online etiquette, and mental wellness in the digital space. Teach them how to apply for jobs online securely, how to handle negative comments with confidence, and how to manage their digital footprint as they grow older.

And remember, your own behavior is your loudest lesson. If you panic every time a problem arises or shame your child for screen-related mistakes, you shut down communication. But if you stay calm, solution-oriented, and empathetic, you create the kind of trust that makes long-term safety possible.

Building a cyber safety culture is not about perfection — it's about consistency. It's about choosing to engage rather than ignore, to teach rather than control, and to empower rather than restrict. When safety becomes a shared mission, not a solo responsibility, everyone in the family wins.

Now, lets go over the a story about the Chen family

The Chen family had always been tech-friendly. Their kids, Leo (age 10) and Maya (age 14), had grown up with tablets, gaming consoles, and smartphones. Dad worked in IT. Mom used her laptop daily for work and online courses. They were a digital household — but recently, things had started to feel... out of sync.

Maya had become secretive with her phone. Leo was addicted to Roblox. Dinner conversations had turned into arguments about screen time. And one night, Maya burst into tears over a TikTok comment – but refused to say what it was. That's when their mom, Aileen, decided something had to change.

Instead of banning devices or tightening the reins, Aileen proposed something new at the breakfast table: "Let's create a family digital plan. Not rules – just values. Things we all agree on, so we can use tech without it using us."

At first, the kids were skeptical. "You're going to make us delete everything," Maya said. "Not at all," Aileen replied. "But we *are* going to start talking about this stuff, together."

That weekend, they gathered in the living room and wrote a "Family Digital Charter" on a poster board. Everyone contributed:

- "No phones at the table." (Leo's idea)
- "Ask before posting photos of each other." (Maya's request)
- "No screens after 9 p.m." (Mom and Dad agreed to join too)

- "If something online makes you feel weird or worried, talk to someone."

They pinned it to the wall beside the fridge. Then, they scheduled "Digital Sundays" — 30-minute family meetings every two weeks to check in about what everyone was watching, playing, or dealing with online. Maya shared how TikTok trends made her anxious. Leo asked why ads kept popping up for things he talked about out loud. Dad explained how phones track data — and showed them how to turn off location tracking.

Soon, the conversations became natural. One evening, Maya came to her mom and said, "A girl at school is being bullied in a group chat. What should I do?" Another night, Leo proudly showed his mom how he ignored a "click here for free Robux" message. He even helped his cousin report a fake gaming account.

The parents led by example. Aileen started leaving her phone in the kitchen at night. Dad removed a few social apps that were draining his time. They both talked openly about how hard it was to stay balanced sometimes — and how important it was to unplug.

The family even created a digital "bucket list" of offline activities they'd try together — hiking, painting, baking, and building a backyard garden. Slowly, the mood in the house shifted. Tech wasn't the enemy — it was just one part of their lives, no longer in control of it.

By the end of the school year, the Chen kids weren't perfect — but they were far more aware. Maya helped her classmates secure their Instagram accounts. Leo started writing stories instead of playing games every afternoon. And when the kids got their report cards, Aileen added a note on the fridge: **"Cyber Safe Champions — Whole Family A+"**

Because in the Chen home, digital safety wasn't a one-time talk. It was a lifestyle — built on trust, teamwork, and the shared goal of growing up smart, strong, and safe in a connected world.

Chapter 9 Title: Preparing Teens for Independent Digital Life

As children grow into teenagers and prepare for adulthood, your role shifts from direct protector to trusted advisor. You've helped them build safe habits, but now it's time to focus on helping them develop **independent digital judgment** – the kind they'll use when they're away from home, out of school, or managing their own devices, finances, and relationships. This chapter is about empowering your teen to think, act, and respond responsibly online – without constant supervision.

Start by transitioning from **rules to values**. At earlier stages, boundaries are about restriction: "No screens after 9 p.m." or "Only approved apps." But as teens mature, values are more effective than commands. These include digital integrity, personal accountability, emotional intelligence, and online empathy. Instead of listing rules, ask:

- "What kind of digital presence do you want to create?"
- "What would you do if someone pressured you to share something private?"
- "How would you respond to a friend posting something you disagree with?"

Encourage them to create their own "digital code" — a short list of principles they agree to live by online. It could include:

- I won't share personal information without thinking twice.
- I won't use anonymous platforms to say things I wouldn't say in person.
- I'll speak up when I see bullying, even if it's uncomfortable.
- I'll take digital breaks when I feel drained or overwhelmed.

Next, begin preparing them for **real-world tech scenarios** they'll soon face:

- **Online purchases**: Teach how to recognize fake stores, secure payment gateways, and the danger of saving card info in unsafe apps.
- **Job applications**: Show them how to scrub inappropriate content from their social media and present themselves professionally online.

- **Public Wi-Fi**: Explain the risks of logging into accounts on unsecured networks and how to use VPNs when necessary.

- **Digital scams**: Review common tactics like fake internship offers, "urgent" password reset emails, and phishing through text or DMs.

Teach them to critically examine **their digital footprint**. Google their name together. What comes up? Are their accounts private or public? Could someone easily find their school, address, or schedule based on posts or photos? This exercise is powerful for showing how the internet remembers — and how to start shaping a more intentional online identity.

Help your teen build **resilience in conflict**. They will eventually face online arguments, exclusion from group chats, ghosting, or even harassment. Instead of telling them what to do, ask:

- "How did that make you feel?"

- "What kind of response do you think is most respectful?"

- "What would you want someone to do if they were in your place?"

This gives them the space to process, reflect, and make better choices. And remind them: walking away, muting, or blocking is often the smartest response – not engaging.

You should also address **digital emotional hygiene** – the regular practice of cleaning up digital clutter and protecting their mental health online. Encourage them to unfollow accounts that make them feel insecure or anxious, delete apps they no longer use, and take regular breaks from platforms that feel overwhelming.

Finally, start including your teen in **family cybersecurity decisions**. Ask them to help set up new devices securely, review Wi-Fi privacy settings, or research password managers with you. Treat them like a partner, not a passive user. This builds confidence and shows that digital responsibility is a life skill – not just a childhood rule.

Preparing your teen for independent digital life doesn't happen overnight. It happens through trust, trial, and growth. They will make mistakes – but those mistakes become teachable moments when you respond with patience instead of panic. The ultimate goal is not just safety, but digital maturity – the ability to make wise decisions even when no one is watching.

The surprise social media story

Seventeen-year-old Jordan was excited to apply for his first internship. It was a paid remote position with a nonprofit, and he'd found it through a post on social media. He clicked the link, uploaded his resume, and filled out a quick form. Within hours, he got a reply: "Congratulations! You've been selected for an interview. Please provide your phone number, full address, and a scanned copy of your student ID."

Something didn't feel right. The email was written in broken English, the sender address looked odd, and the website had disappeared when he tried to revisit it. So, for the first time, Jordan decided to ask his dad, Marcus, for help.

Marcus listened carefully and praised Jordan for his instincts. Together, they looked up the company and found a warning on a job scam database — the post was fake. Jordan exhaled, relieved. "I almost gave them everything," he said. "It felt real."

That night, they talked for hours. Marcus didn't scold or shame him. Instead, he said, "This is the kind of thing that happens to everyone — even adults. What matters is what we learn." He showed Jordan how to spot phishing emails, verify websites, and use a secondary email address for job applications.

The next day, they reviewed Jordan's social media. "If an employer googles you," Marcus asked, "what do they see?" Jordan's TikTok was full of memes, harmless but silly. His Instagram had a few edgy captions. "Nothing terrible," Marcus said, "but maybe not what you'd want to lead with." Jordan nodded. They set his accounts to private and created a LinkedIn profile instead — clean, professional, and honest.

A few weeks later, Jordan received a real job offer. This time, he was ready. He reviewed the sender's domain, searched the company's leadership, and asked smart questions in the interview. "Thanks for teaching me how to check things out," he told his dad afterward. "I feel like I actually know what I'm doing now."

Their conversations deepened. One night, Jordan told Marcus about a group chat that turned mean — friends teasing another kid behind his back. "What should I do?" he asked. Marcus didn't give orders. He asked, "What do you think is the right thing?" After a long pause, Jordan said, "I think I'll leave the chat. And maybe check in with the kid they're targeting."

Little by little, Jordan started owning his choices. He muted notifications during study hours. He deleted a few apps he found draining. He even helped his younger sister set up her new tablet — making sure privacy settings were locked down.

At graduation, Marcus smiled watching Jordan speak to his class. "The world's complicated," Jordan said in his speech, "but we've got the tools to figure it out — online and off."

It was clear: Jordan wasn't just tech-savvy. He was *digitally mature*. And his journey started the moment someone trusted him to learn, rather than just follow rules.

Epilogue: Raising Digital Citizens for a Safer Tomorrow

The goal of this guide has never been to scare you or overwhelm you. It's been to equip you. Because parenting in the digital age requires something more than device restrictions and password protection — it requires a shift in mindset. Our children aren't just using technology — they're growing up in it. They're building relationships, learning, expressing themselves, and shaping their identity inside this digital world. And that means we, as parents and caregivers, must evolve alongside them.

Cyber safety is no longer about temporary fixes. It's a way of life. It's the language we speak around the dinner table when we ask what our kids saw online that day. It's the routine we build when we put phones away during family time or talk openly about feelings triggered by social media. It's the culture we establish when we celebrate smart choices, question viral trends, and support our kids through their mistakes — not shame them.

Yes, there are dangers — cyberbullying, predators, scams, exposure to inappropriate content, addiction. But there are also opportunities — to connect across cultures, to learn from the world's greatest teachers, to find mentors, to build communities, to create. Our job isn't to shut our kids away from technology — it's to teach them how to live in it wisely, intentionally, and confidently.

If you've followed each chapter, you now have a foundation:

- You understand the digital worlds your kids live in.
- You know how to establish healthy boundaries that don't break trust.
- You've explored tools for parental control and how to gradually release responsibility.
- You've learned how to teach critical thinking and support emotional health in the digital space.
- You've seen how to build a home culture where cyber safety is a shared, ongoing value.
- And most importantly, you've started shifting your role — from rule-setter to digital mentor.

You don't need to have all the answers. You don't need to be a cybersecurity expert. You just need to be involved, informed, and willing to grow. Because the greatest protection your child has isn't software — it's *you*. Your presence, your interest, your willingness to listen and learn with them. That's what makes the difference.

Moving forward, continue to adapt. New platforms will emerge. New threats will evolve. But so will new opportunities to connect, create, and contribute. Stay curious. Keep asking your kids about their favorite apps, new games, or online experiences. Let them teach you. And when something goes wrong — because something eventually will — be the safe space they return to.

One day, they'll be on their own. They'll make decisions about sharing, posting, replying, trusting — without you there. But the values you've instilled, the conversations you've had, the example you've modeled — these will guide them. They will carry your voice in their mind: *"Is this safe? Is this smart? Will this help or hurt me?"*

And maybe — just maybe — they'll pass those same lessons on to their own children one day.

In the end, this isn't just about protecting your child's devices. It's about protecting their dignity, their future, their confidence in who they are — online and offline. And that is a mission worth committing to every single day.

Before we finish, let's talk about the Flores family and their story

It was a warm Sunday evening, and the Flores family was gathered around the backyard fire pit. The kids, Nia (16) and Dylan (12), were roasting marshmallows while their parents, Miguel and Janessa, talked about the week ahead. For once, no one was on their phone. No screens, no background music – just stories, laughter, and stars.

Earlier that day, Dylan had helped his dad update the home Wi-Fi security settings. Nia had shown her mom how to enable two-factor authentication on her social media. These moments had become part of life now – normal, not forced.

It hadn't always been that way. There had been arguments, boundary-setting, mistakes – like the time Nia clicked on a fake scholarship ad, or when Dylan got into a heated gaming chat and said something he regretted. But each time, instead of punishing, Miguel and Janessa leaned in. They turned incidents into lessons. Conversations replaced lectures. Trust replaced fear.

Over time, something incredible happened: the kids began managing their own screen time. They started asking themselves questions before posting. They chose better passwords. They began noticing when certain content made them anxious and took breaks. Not because a rule said so — but because they'd learned to recognize the signs and listen to themselves.

Nia even led a workshop at school called "Think Before You Click." Dylan created a poster about phishing scams for his class project. And at home, they all worked together to create new tech traditions — like "Digital-Free Fridays" and an annual "Cyber Spring Clean," where they reviewed accounts, deleted old apps, and set new intentions.

That night by the fire, Miguel looked at his family and felt something rare in the age of hyperconnectivity: peace. He realized they weren't just surviving digital life — they were thriving in it. They had created a home where mistakes were met with grace, where questions were encouraged, and where everyone had a voice in how technology was used.

Janessa turned to the kids and asked, "What's one thing you've learned this year about being online?"

Dylan said, "That not everything is what it seems. And it's okay to walk away."

Nia added, "That privacy is power. And I get to decide how much of me the internet sees."

Miguel and Janessa smiled.

They didn't have all the answers. But they had something better — a family culture where digital life was talked about, navigated together, and shaped by love, not fear.

And in that moment, under the stars, with sticky fingers and full hearts, they knew: their children were ready.

Not to be perfect.

But to be *prepared.*

www.ingramcontent.com/pod-product-compliance
Lightning Source LLC
LaVergne TN
LVHW022024200926
848481LV00007B/2536